Chinese Celebrations

FOR CHILDREN

Festivals, Holidays and Traditions

text by Susan Miho Nunes
illustrations by Patrick Yee

TUTTLE Publishing

Tokyo | Rutland, Vermont | Singapore

Let's Celebrate!

Chinese people love celebrations. Wherever we make our home, people celebrate on special days. Families gather, sometimes traveling great distances to be together. They honor their ancestors, remember them with offerings of thanks. They mark the changing seasons and share delicious foods made especially for that occasion. When a whole community celebrates together, the celebration becomes a festival.

Chinese Festivals

Chinese festivals have a long history with roots in agriculture, legend, and myth. People celebrated with festivals even in bad times, because the activities offered hope for the future. Although many customs are shared today, there is no single way to celebrate. China is a big country, and customs can vary from province to province, city to city, family to family. Chinese people live all over the world and have shaped these occasions in different ways.

Gifts

A gift is a way to keep up ties—to elders, relatives and friends.

Family Gatherings

Celebrations are family affairs. Family activities highlight many Chinese holidays. People enjoy celebrating together, sharing food and stories and good will. People are willing to travel great distances to be with loved ones who live far apart.

Let's Follow the Moon!

Celebrations and the Chinese Calendar

The solar calendar follows the earth's movement around the sun. The lunar calendar follows the moon's cycle around the earth. Most of the celebrations in this book follow the Xia, or lunar, calendar. One moon cycle takes a little less than thirty days. Twelve moon cycles make up a year.

Fireworks!

Fireworks are used to celebrate all kinds of joyful occasions. They are beautiful and festive, and the lights and noise chase away evil spirits.

Chinese Almanac

The Chinese Almanac tells which days in the coming year will be most auspicious. Many people plan for activities like weddings and travel to take place on these lucky dates.

To Celebrate 祝贺

These days the people of China and most of East Asia follow the Western, or Gregorian, calendar for day-to-day activities. But they turn to the lunar calendar for their traditional celebrations and also for choosing other important and auspicious dates, such as weddings.

New Year's Eve Chu Xi (除夕)

Last Day of the Lunar Year (January or February)

Beginning at the end...

As the old year draws to a close, all over China and around the globe millions of people take to the roads, seas and skies and travel home to their families. Everyone is in a rush to arrive before the big dinner on the very last day of the year. This travel season is so important that it has its own name: *Chun Yun*.

Meanwhile, people at home are busy getting everything ready before midnight on the last day of the year. The New Year must be welcomed with a clean slate. Debts must be paid, disagreements settled, the house scrubbed from top to bottom to remove all traces of bad luck, and offerings must be made to the Kitchen God.

"*Gong Xi Fa Cai*!" Wishing you prosperity!

Welcome the guests! The gods and family ancestors partake of the feast and quietly depart. Then the family sits down to enjoy the feast.

Gods of the Household, Heavens and Fortune

The Jade Emperor
Yu Huang (玉皇)
Rules the heavens and the universe

The Three Lucky Gods
Fu Lu Shou (福禄寿)

| God of Fortune and Happiness Fu Xing (福星) | God of Prosperity Lu Xing (禄星) | God of Longevity Shou Xing (寿星) |

God of Wealth
Tsai Shen (财神)
Brings blessings and prosperity to the New Year.

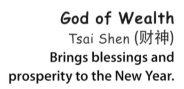

The Kitchen God
Zao Shen (灶神)
Watches over the household. Also known as the stove god.

Goddess of Compassion
Guan Yin (观音)
Known for her mercy, love and kindness.

Before the New Year begins, here are some things to do... and not to do:

Things to Do

- Put up posters of the household gods
- Put up New Year's posters (nianhua) and good luck sayings (chun lian)
- Clean the house and sweep away misfortune
- Make offerings to the Kitchen God
- Burn paper effigies
- Decorate windows with red paper cutouts and little verses to good fortune
- Shop for new clothes
- Buy food and gifts
- Prepare a New Year's Eve feast

Things Not to Do

- Do not cry
- Do not break anything
- Do not borrow money
- Do not say unlucky words

New Year's Eve Dinner

Eating special dishes brings good luck in the coming year.

1. Turnip Cakes Luo Bo Gao

The name for turnip cake (Luo Bo Gao) is associated with good luck.

2. Buddha's Delight Luo Han Zhai

A vegetable dish containing black algae, pronounced "fat choy" in Cantonese, which means prosperity.

3. Mandarin Oranges Jin Ju

Gold fruit to bring luck and fortune.

4. New Year Cakes Nian Gao

A pudding made of rice flour, wheat starch, salt, water and sugar, popular in Eastern China. Its name sounds like the greeting, "A more prosperous year."

5. Taro Cakes

Like nian gao, this savory treat means "to improve" every year.

6. Noodles

Serve them very long for a long life.

7. Dried Barbecued Jerky Bakkwa

Salty sweet dried meat. In Southern China and Singapore, this is a special treat often given as a gift. Meat was once difficult to preserve and so is very precious.

8. Jao Gok

A dumpling made to look like an ancient bar of gold.

9. Yu Sheng or Yae Sang

A raw fish salad popular in places like Singapore. Toss it high for auspicious wishes!

10. Dumpling Jiao Zi

In Northern China, a dumpling with good luck packaged inside.

11. Fish

The word for fish sounds like the word for "surplus."

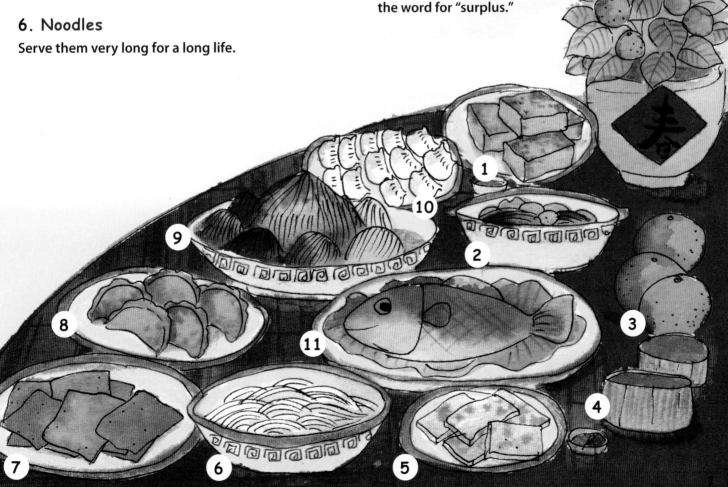

Fireworks!

The sound of fireworks awakens the sleeping dragon, who brings the spring rain to water the crops each year.

Chinese New Year Chūn Jié (春节)

1st Day of the 1st Lunar Month (January or February)

Spring Festival Is Here!

A big burst of firecrackers signals the end of the old year and the start of the new. People pour into the streets. They exchange greetings, bows, and handshakes. The new zodiac animal has begun the new cycle. The long-awaited Spring Festival has begun!

The New Year Is In!

After a night of celebrating, children wake up and greet their parents with wishes for a healthy and happy new year. They receive red paper envelopes with money inside. All grudges are forgiven. Peace, harmony and joy rule the day.

Xin Nian Hao!

Happy New Year!

Gong He Xin Xi!

All the food has been cooked and prepared the day before. Clothes have been bought, hair has been cut and the house has been cleaned.

Dragon Dances!

Dancing dragons bring good luck. They liven Chinese festivals throughout the year, but at this time they are especially welcome.

Lion Dances!

The lion signifies courage and strength. The lion's dance chases away ghosts and evil spirits. Because evil spirits are afraid of loud noises, the lion's dance is accompanied by the explosion of firecrackers and the beat of drums.

Steps in the Lion's Dance:

- Pays respects at the temple
- Moves through streets bringing joy and happiness
- Stops to chew green leaves strung from shop windows
- Spits out leaves
- Allows brave people to stick their heads into his mouth

Head, twinkling eyelids, mouth, mirror to expel bad energy

Tail, sweeps away bad luck

Two performers, head and tail

During Chinese New Year

Families visit the oldest and most senior members of the family—parents, grandparents, great-grandparents.

Red and Gold Are Everywhere

- Red and gold stand for good luck and prosperity.
- Red envelopes. For the children, money in even numbers
- Red clothes.
- Red decorations…lanterns, paper cutouts.
- Firecrackers rolled in red paper.
- Mandarin oranges…gold for prosperity.

Spring Calligraphy

Try your hand at writing characters for this special season. Spring. Good Luck. Prosperity. Happiness. See page 17 for more ideas. And don't forget to hang up your work!

WHAT YOU NEED:

Red construction paper square 8"x 8"
Cardboard square, same size, for backing
White paper squares, 6" x 6"
Pencil for tracing
Wide tip black felt pen (or calligraphy brush and ink)
Scissors
Glue
Hole punch
String or ribbon for hanging up

HOW YOU MAKE THEM:

1. Cut red paper square. Cut cardboard square for backing.
2. Glue red square to cardboard backing.
3. Trace character on white square (with pencil). Finish off with black pen.
4. Or, draw or copy the character with calligraphy brush
5. Paste white square (with character) on red square.
6. Punch hole on top of red square
7. Attach string or ribbon and tie in loop.
8. Hang up your work!

The Legend of Nian

Once long ago in the farming villages of China, a fearsome creature called Nian began to appear on the eve of the New Year. He had fiery eyes, lots of teeth, and a great horn on his forehead. He ate the crops and livestock—sometimes even the children! The villagers were so frightened that they would leave their homes before the eve of the New Year and hide in the mountains. They would return after the New Year and find everything eaten or destroyed. What should have been a joyful time became a time of hardship and pain.

One New Year's eve as the villagers prepared to flee, a beggar appeared and asked for a place to stay. The villagers told him, "The Nian is coming! We are going to hide in the mountains. You cannot stay here, or you will be eaten."

The beggar replied, "If you give me a night's shelter, I promise to help you drive this Nian away."

Still frightened, but tired of running away every year, the villagers gave him a place to stay. "What shall we do about Nian?" they asked.

The beggar told them, "Hang red papers over your doors. Light all the lanterns in your houses. Dress your children in new clothes. Gather your drums and gongs. When you hear Nian coming, beat on them as loudly as you can."

The villagers rushed about following the beggar's instructions. And then they waited. When the eve came, Nian roared into the village as usual. But this time, to his surprise, he found it ablaze with lanterns. Everywhere he turned he faced doorways bright with red paper. And children running around in red clothes. From every street and alley came the deafening noise of drums and gongs. Now it was Nian's turn to flee to the mountains.

It is said that eventually the ancient monk Hongjun Laozu captured and tamed the ferocious Nian. But still, every New Year's Eve, people decorate their homes with red paper and lighted lanterns. They dress their children in red clothes. And they set off fireworks and beat on gongs and drums—just in case!

The Chinese Zodiac Sheng Xiao (生肖)

The zodiac calendar repeats itself every twelve years. Each year is named after one of twelve animals. Many Chinese still believe these animal characters influence the personalities of people born in their particular year. They say, "That is the animal that hides in your heart."

It is said that the gods decreed that a great race across the river would decide the order of the animals in the zodiac. The ox worried about his poor eyesight and the rat offered to ride on his back and be his eyes. When they reached the shore, the clever rat hopped off the ox's back to be the winner of the race.

The Five Elements
Wood, fire, earth, metal, and water all work together

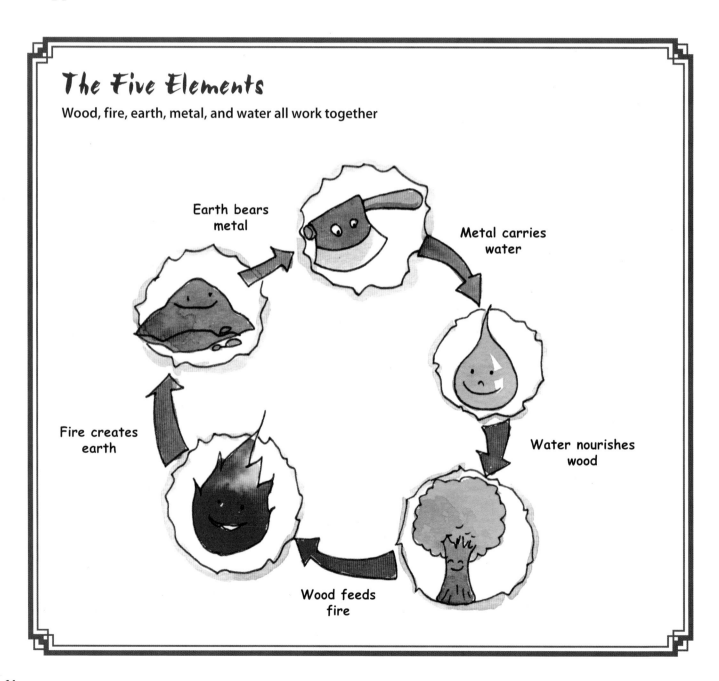

Earth bears metal

Metal carries water

Water nourishes wood

Wood feeds fire

Fire creates earth

Chart Showing Years & Animals

The zodiac has 12 animals. But instead of beginning a new cycle every 12 years, the Chinese assign one of the five elements to an animal each year. This creates 60 different combinations. Thus the years pass in 60-year cycles, with each year having a unique combination of animal and element.

The 60-year cycle

Zi Shu

The rat is sensitive, charming, and hard working.

Chou Niu

The ox is patient, dependable and steady.

Yin Hu

The tiger is powerful, daring, and generous.

Mao Tu

The rabbit is kind, elegant, and compassionate.

Chen Long

The dragon is noble, strong and proud.

Si She

The snake is wise, creative, and thoughtful.

Wu Ma

The horse is cheerful, popular, and open-minded.

Wei Yang

The ram is generous, understanding and peaceful.

Shen Hou

The monkey is curious, motivated, and friendly.

You Ji

The rooster is neat, organized, and confident.

Xu Gou or Quan

The dog is honest, intelligent and loyal.

Hai Zhu or Tun

The pig is patient, calm, and intelligent.

Lunar Chinese New Year

This is the longest and most important celebration in the year. It is celebrated all over the world, wherever Chinese people have made their homes: Mainland China, Hong Kong and Macao, Taiwan, Christmas Island, Malaysia, and other overseas Chinese communities.

New Year's Cards

New Year's Cards are an important Chinese tradition. The cards may have the year's zodiac symbol printed on them, or they may have one of these lucky symbols to wish the recipient a happy, lucky New Year.

HOW YOU MAKE THEM:

1. Make your own cards, using red and gold paper and adding your own best wishes!

2. Fold paper in half

3. Decorate with a character, or lucky symbol

4. Lanterns, or

5. Zodiac symbol, and

6. Write your own best wishes inside!

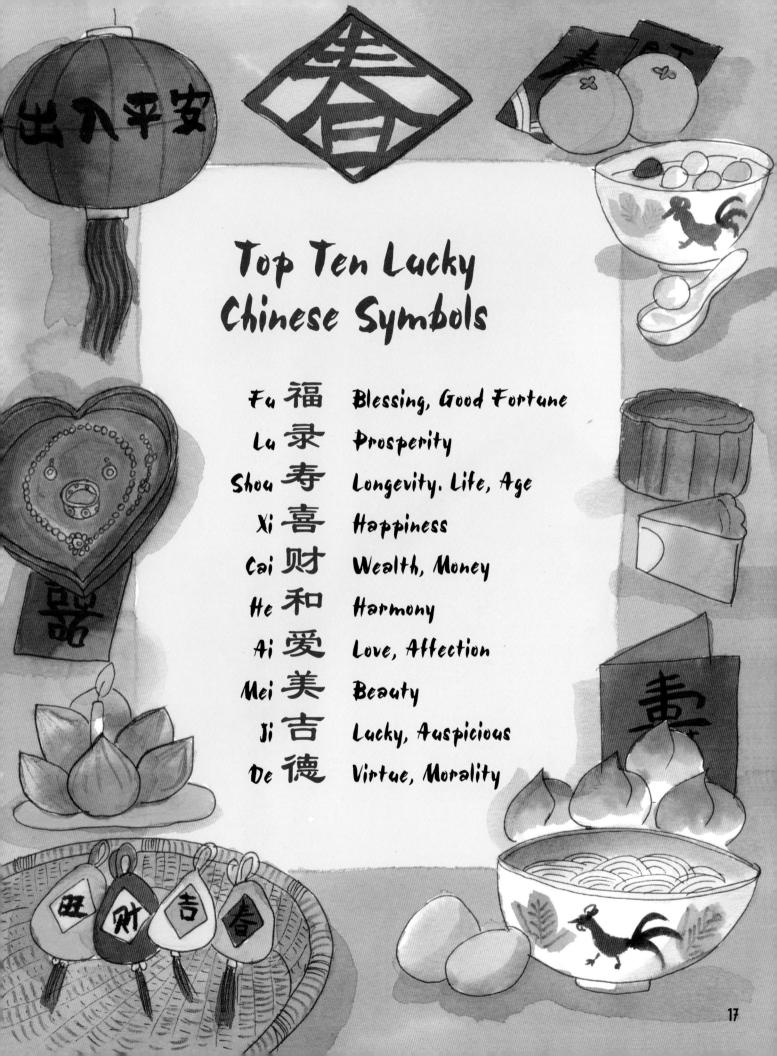

Top Ten Lucky Chinese Symbols

Fu	福	Blessing, Good Fortune
Lu	录	Prosperity
Shou	寿	Longevity, Life, Age
Xi	喜	Happiness
Cai	财	Wealth, Money
He	和	Harmony
Ai	爱	Love, Affection
Mei	美	Beauty
Ji	吉	Lucky, Auspicious
De	德	Virtue, Morality

The Days of the Spring Festival

The Spring Festival lasts for fifteen days, after the Lunar New Year. After the celebrations of the first day, certain other days have special activities.

Second Day

- Burn incense and offer prayers at the graves of ancestors
- Married daughters, visit your birth parents
- Feed dogs well, for this day is their birthday

Third Day

- Stay home to avoid the "God of Blazing Wrath"

Fifth Day

- Eat dumplings in the morning
- Celebrate the birthday of Guan Yu, the God of Wealth
- Firecrackers might get his attention

Seventh Day

- Everyone is a year older. Celebrate!
- Enjoy Yu Sheng, tossed raw fish salad, to bring good luck

Ninth Day

- Offer prayers to the Jade Emperor on his birthday

Thirteenth Day

Eat pure vegetarian food to recover from the rich diet of the previous days, Honor Guan Yu, the God of War and the greatest general in Chinese history

Fifteenth Day

Light the lanterns!

The Lantern Festival Yuan Xiao (元宵)

15th Day of the 1st Lunar Month in February on the Last Day of the Spring Festival

It's Time to Light the Lanterns.

The beautiful Lantern Festival marks the last day of the Spring Festival and the day when the first full moon enters the new year. At night, people fill streets that are ablaze with lanterns of every shape, color, and size—insects, butterflies, dragons, fish, and snakes. Whole families walk the streets holding lanterns. Crowds gather to watch lantern parades and lion dances. Sometimes a dragon will appear. People feast on *tangyuan*, a sweet, stuffed rice dumpling.

Lantern Parade

Let us watch the parade of lanterns, joined by stilt-walkers, dragons, lions and other exciting sights.

Wishes
Write your wishes on your lanterns.

- Good health!
- Onward!
- Be happy!
- Pass your exams!
- Work smoothly!
- Good luck!

Colors
Symbolic colors help wishes come true.

Red: Good Fortune

Pink: Romance

Peach: Opportunity

Orange: Money

Yellow: Success

White: Health

Green: Growth

Light Blue: Hope for something wished for

Light Purple: Idealism

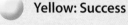

Lantern Riddles

Tricky riddles are written on the lanterns. In big celebrations, you can win a prize for guessing the answers. Can you guess the answers to these riddles?

When you wash, it's dirty.
When you don't wash, it's clean.

Ans: water

Two boats with five guests in each, sail on land but never on water. They are busy in the daytime, but anchored at night.

Ans: Shoes

Red Paper Lanterns

Lanterns festoon shops and homes, hang from fences and are strung across courtyards and restaurants. Some lanterns have puzzles and riddles written on them. Guessing these lantern riddles is an important part of the festivities. You may win a prize for the right answer.

Make a Paper Lantern

Make a paper lantern for your lantern festival. Or, make several and string them across the room.

WHAT YOU NEED:

- Colored construction paper
- Scissors
- Glue
- Tape or Stapler (optional)
- Gold Glitter

1. Fold paper in half lengthwise.

2. Make a series of cuts along the fold line (about ¾" apart) Be careful not to cut all the way to the edge.

3. Unfold. Glue or staple short edges together.

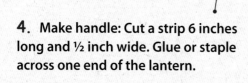

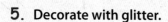

4. Make handle: Cut a strip 6 inches long and ½ inch wide. Glue or staple across one end of the lantern.

5. Decorate with glitter.

6. Make many and string across the room!

Celebrating Lantern Festival in a Parade

Lantern Festival days are full of lion dances, dragon dances and moon watching. In countries like Malaysia and Singapore, the Lantern Festival is like Valentine's Day.

Dragon Lantern Dances

A dragon ablaze with lights dances down the street. Sometimes people holding lanterns can form the long body of the dragon.

Stilt Walking

An ancient art performed for the delight of young and old. The walking skill, which takes much practice and daring to master, has also been turned into beautiful dances.

Sweet Glutinous Rice Balls

Tangyuan, (also called yuanxiao). These delicious dumplings are made of rice flour and may be filled with rose petals, bean paste, walnut meat, dried fruit. They can be boiled, fried, or steamed. They are sweet and delicious.

Names on Oranges

It is the custom in some places for a young woman to write her name on an orange and set it afloat. If a young man finds the orange and it is sweet, the couple's fate will be good.

Sweet Glutinous Rice Balls Tangyuan

This colorful and delicious dish looks and tastes like a celebration. It is fun to make and a pleasure to share.

YOU WILL NEED:

For Sweet Soup

4 cups water
2 pandan leaves, tied in knot
2-inch piece ginger, peeled and
   slightly crushed
½ c. superfine (or regular) white sugar

Water

Pandan Leaves

For Dumplings

2 cups glutinous rice flour
1 tablespoon superfine white sugar
1 cup water (more or less)
Assorted food coloring

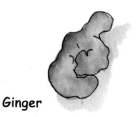
Ginger

Regular White Sugar

Glutinous
Rice Flour

Water

Superfine
White Sugar

Assorted food
coloring

HOW TO MAKE THE SWEET SOUP:

1. Make your sweet soup. With adult help, bring water to boil.

2. Add pandan leaves and ginger.

3. Boil 5 minutes till you smell the aroma.

4. Add sugar. Turn down heat and simmer uncovered for 15 minutes.

5. Remove leaves and ginger. Set soup aside.

Hints:

When mixing dumplings, if dough is too wet, add more flour; if too dry, add more water. Pandan leaves can be found in Asian markets. If you can't find them, your syrup will still be fine.

HOW TO MAKE THE DUMPLINGS:

1. Make your dumplings. Put glutinous rice flour and sugar in mixing bowl.

2. Slowly add water and knead to form dough, adding more water as you work. When dough no longer sticks to hands, it's ready (about 5 minutes).

3. Divide dough into 3 or 4 parts.

4. Add 2-3 drops of coloring to each part, knead to blend color. Pinch off pieces of dough and roll into small, bite-sized balls.

5. With adult help, heat a pot of water to boiling, drop balls into water and cook until balls rise to surface (about 5-7 minutes).

6. Place cooked balls in sweet soup and serve!

Dragon Head-Raising Day Long Tai Tou

2nd Day of the 2nd Lunar Month (February or March)

According to legend, on this day the dragon king awakens and raises his head. Farmers in Northern China believed that once he awoke, the rain would fall and harvests would be full.

In northern China, farmers carry lanterns to the wells and rivers to pay tribute to the dragon king. They light candles and burn incense. They eat spring pancakes, *chun bing*, filled with good things. And they make popcorn!

In south China, this day is known as Ta Qing Jie, Step-on-the-Grass Day. Green, the color of Spring, is the color of the day.

Ancient Taboos

Be sure to cut your hair. Get rid of the old and embrace the new.
No needles, please. One might harm the dragon's eyes.
"Wear the dragon's tail" with colorful pieces of cloth.
"Load the dragon's eggs" by fetching water early in the morning.

Special Foods

Special foods are given dragon names.

Dragon's ears—dumplings

Dragon's scales—pancakes

Welcome the Dragon Dances

Dragon dances in the street invite good luck and ensure a plentiful harvest.

Hair Cut Taboo
Get rid of the old and embrace the new

Dragon's beard—noodles

The Story of the Golden Bean

In a far distant time, everyone paid tribute to the Dragon at the start of spring, for he was the bringer of life, peace and prosperity. When, after his winter sleep, he raised his head again, rain would fall and grass would grow. Among the ancient rituals to honor the Dragon, kings would work in the fields and queens would cook for the poor. But in time, people grew afraid to sew or plow at festival time, for fear of poking out the dragon's eyes or scratching his skin.

One day an empress who disliked the ancient practices banned the festival. The Emperor of Heaven became angry and sent three years of drought. The Jade Dragon took pity on the suffering people and let the rain fall. This infuriated the Emperor even more, and he punished the Dragon by burying him under a mountain, refusing to release him until the golden bean flowered.

To rescue the dragon, the people searched for the golden bean, to no avail. One day, they realized that kernels of corn resembled golden beans. When popped, the kernels looked like flowers.

They piled heaps of kernels and popped corn on their altars. The Emperor of Heaven kept his word and released the Dragon. Ever since, people have enjoyed popcorn on this day.

Shangsi Festival

3ʀᴅ Day of the 3ʀᴅ Lunar Month (March or April)

This ancient festival is sometimes called Double Third Festival because it takes place on the third day of the third month of the Chinese calendar. Traditional activities honored ancestors and the Goddess of Marriage and Childbearing. Though customs have changed over the years, many activities are still associated with flowing water and its cleansing properties. Special things to do on this day include having picnics by the water, gathering orchids, and floating eggs down the river.

Pray for Children

Couples honor the Goddess of Marriage and Childbearing.

Pick Orchids

Among outdoor activities, picking flowers in the fields is still a favorite

Meet Friends

In some communities, people celebrate this day as a festival of love. Picnics and other gatherings are opportunities for young people to get to know each other.

Picnics by Waterside

Families and young couples gather by the river to share a meal, tell stories, enjoy one another's company. In the old days, people honored their ancestors and then bathed in the river to remove evil spirits.

Float eggs and wine cups

An old tradition expresses the wish for many children.

Pure Brightness Day Qing Ming Jie

104 Days after the Winter Solstice (Around April 5th)

The Chinese word for this day means clear and bright. On this day Spring has definitely arrived. Today Qing Ming is a day to remember one's ancestors. Graves are swept, cleaned, and decorated with fresh greenery and flowers. Incense and paper money or other tokens of wealth are burned as offerings. Dishes of food and fruit are served. Firecrackers add to the ceremony in which whole families take part.
In this way, families keep alive their links to ancestors.

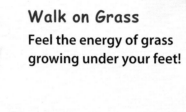

Walk on Grass

Feel the energy of grass growing under your feet!

Other Names

Tomb Sweeping Day, Mourning Day, Walking on Greenery Day.

Go on a Spring Outing

After a long winter, it's a pleasure to be outside on a bright, sunny spring day.

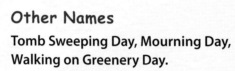

Plant Trees

Qing Ming is a festival of beautiful flowers and green trees.

Fly a Kite

A kite flying on a spring breeze lifts winter spirits.

About Kites

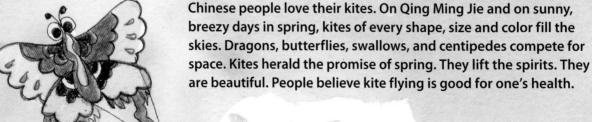

Chinese people love their kites. On Qing Ming Jie and on sunny, breezy days in spring, kites of every shape, size and color fill the skies. Dragons, butterflies, swallows, and centipedes compete for space. Kites herald the promise of spring. They lift the spirits. They are beautiful. People believe kite flying is good for one's health.

Dragon Boat Festival Duan Wu Jie

5th Day of the 5th Lunar Month (May or June)

The Dragon Boat Festival marks the beginning of summer when the daylight is longest. Traditionally, the dragon and the sun were connected, and the festival goes back more than two thousand years. It has been a public holiday in China since 2008. In Hong Kong and Macao it is known by the Cantonese name *Tuen Ng Jit*.

People race dragon boats and eat rice dumplings called zongzi. For good health, they wear perfumed medicine bags, hang medicinal leaves from doors and windows, or take long walks. Some people play a game of making an egg stand up at noon.

31

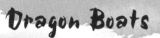

Dragon Boats

Shaped to look like dragons, the boats come in all sizes, from ten paddlers to more than fifty, though most boats have twenty. A drummer sits at the bow, facing the paddlers. The person steering sits at the rear. The sound of the drum, which keeps the pace of paddling, represents the dragon's heartbeat.

The Story of Qu Yuan

Qu Yuan was a poet, a scholar, and a statesman who lived some 2,300 years ago in the ancient state of Chu. Under threat from a neighboring state, he advised his leaders how to defend the country against invaders. He was opposed by rivals and eventually exiled.

On the fifth day of the fifth moon in the year 295 B.C., he plunged into the Milo River in Hunan Province. People rushed to their boats and searched for him in vain. It is said that every year on this day, people would row their boats into the local waterways and throw bamboo stems filled with rice into the water in remembrance. Today, dragon boat festivals are held all over China and other parts of the world to honor the spirit of Qu Yuan.

Offering Dumplings
Qu Yuan is not forgotten. On festival days, people enjoy zongzi, traditional triangular dumplings of glutinous rice wrapped in bamboo leaves.

The Night of Sevens Qixi Festival

7th Day of the 7th Lunar Month (August)

North and south on the Milky Way, two bright stars seem to be signaling each other without pause. Here is their story marking the Night of Sevens Festival, the most romantic of the yearly festivals and traditionally the most valued by girls.

The Qixi Festival is also known as the Double Seventh Festival, Ingenuity-Begging Festival, and the Magpie Festival.

Floating a Needle

On this day, it's a tradition for girls to lay a needle on a bowl of water to see if it floats—if it does, the girl will be a good needlewoman.

Girls Make Offerings to the Gods

In traditional times to mark the annual reunion of the weaver girl and the cowherd, girls would go to the temples to pray for wisdom, for a good husband, and for dexterity in needlework. Today, girls still burn paper items as offerings and pray for a good marriage.

Chinese Valentine's Day

It is a tradition at this time to look at the sky and search for Vega and Altair, the stars that represent the mythical couple whose love endured despite times of heartbreaking separation.

The Cowherd and the Weaver Maid

Niu Lang, orphaned as a boy, lived alone as a cowherd. Zhi Nu, daughter of the Goddess of Heaven, was charged with weaving colorful clouds. One day she ventured down to earth, met Niu Lang, fell in love and married him. He farmed, she wove, and they raised two children. They were a happy family.

The Queen of Heaven disapproved and ordered the Weaver Maid home. Helped by celestial cattle, Niu Lang flew to heaven with his children. Just as he was about to reach her, the Queen formed a river in the sky to block his way.

Moved by Niu Lang's plight, magpies by the thousands formed a bridge over the river so that the family could reunite for one day each year.

Each year, on the seventh day of the seventh month the magpies are said to form a bridge over the Milky Way so that the cowherd and weaver maid may meet again.

Magpie
Asian magpies are in the same bird family as ravens and crows. They are black, with white breast feathers and long tails. People believe magpies bring good fortune and joy, and because they united Niu Lang and Zhi Nu, they have come to symbolize a happy marriage.

Spirit Festival or Ghost Festival

Zhongyuan Jie

15ᵗʰ Day of the 7ᵗʰ Lunar Month (August or September)

Chinese people do not forget those who have left this world. On this day families make offerings to wandering spirits and burn fake paper money to help spirits on their journey. At sundown, whole families can be seen at riverside or seashore setting lighted lanterns adrift. The lanterns are in the shape of flowers. How beautiful they are, carried downstream or away from shore! The Chinese feast to help hungry ghosts is a bountiful spread. No ghost leaves hungry! In Chinese Buddhism, the celebration is called Yulan Jie. Many of the customs have origins in the story of Mu Lian.

Offerings to Gods

People offer food, incense, and prayers to the gods of heaven, earth, and water, who have the power to bestow happiness, pardon sins, and provide protection.

Burning Incense and Paper

People burn paper money, joss paper, and replicas of real items, like cars and clothes. The practice is done outside the home.

Floating Water Lanterns Guide Souls

In some places, people release water lanterns on the rivers on the night of the fourteenth day. They can be elaborate or simple, but they are always beautiful.

The Story Of Mu Lian

Mu Lian was devoted to his mother. As a young man he left home to receive spiritual training, even though his mother begged him to stay. Years later, when he completed his training and returned home, he discovered that his mother had died.

In sorrow for neglecting his mother, he meditated in the hope of seeing her. He learned that because she had been wicked in this life, she could not move on to the next. She begged him for food, but because no one had prayed for her or done penance on her behalf, she was unworthy to eat the food he offered.

Mu Lian sought wisdom from his teacher, who told him that to make his mother worthy to eat again he should first feed the living. When he had fed thousands, his mother was able to eat the food offered to her. Later, after many years of sacrifice and spiritual living, Mu Lian won his mother's right to move onward.

The Chinese love this story for its happy ending and its lesson on respect and duty to one's parents. Among the Chinese, this is considered one of the greatest of all virtues.

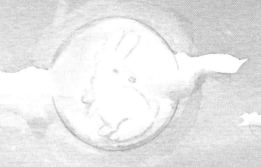

Jade Rabbit

When the moon in its fullest brilliance, children are sure to hear the story of the fairy living on the moon in an icy crystal palace. Her only companion is a jade rabbit. She may have an occasional visitor and dance for the company, but otherwise she is alone. In other versions, she is the moon goddess, and her rabbit companion mixes the elixir of life for her with his pestle and mortar.

Mid Autumn Festival Zhongqiu Jie

15th Day of the 8th Lunar Month (September or October)

This festival celebrates the fullness of the autumn moon. On this important holiday families gather to enjoy a meal, gaze at the moon and eat mooncakes.

Family Gatherings

One of the highlights of the Moon Festival is when families gather to eat a moonlit meal and share some of the many legends associated with this holiday.

Mooncakes

Traditionally, the mooncakes were filled with lotus seed paste and a salted egg yoke in the center. Today, fillings include red bean paste, mixed nuts, dried fruits, and even ham.

The Story of Hou Yi

Hou Yi was an officer of the Emperor's Imperial Guards, and a brilliant archer. When ten suns suddenly appeared in the sky, the emperor ordered him to shoot all but one out of the sky. This Hou Yi did with great skill.

As a reward, the Goddess of the Western Heaven asked Hou Yi to build her a palace of jade. His work so pleased the goddess that she gave him the gift of everlasting life in a little pill he was to swallow after a year of fasting and prayer. He took the pill home and hid it.

Hou Yi's wife, a beautiful woman named Chang E, found the hidden pill and, in her curiosity, swallowed it. Punishment was swift. As Chang E floated away, her husband tried to save her, but was swept back by sudden winds.

Storytellers say that Chang E's radiant beauty makes the moon even more beautiful. Listeners must surely think of her as they enjoy tea and mooncakes at the Mid Autumn Moon Festival.

Double Ninth Festival Chong Yang Jie

9th Day of the 9th Lunar Month (October)

The clear, cool days of the ninth month make it a good time for outings. On *Chong Yang Jie*, families spend the day hiking in the hills, viewing chrysanthemums, drinking chrysanthemum wine, and eating Double Ninth cakes. It is a special day for the elderly.

The word *chong* means double. The word *yang*, which in ancient China was associated with the number 9, has the meaning masculine or positive. As the words for "double nine" are pronounced the same as the word for "forever," here was a perfect meeting of words and meanings. This day is worthy of celebration!

Make a Paper Chrysanthemum

The chrysanthemum is said to have purifying qualities and is the special flower of the Double Ninth Festival. Try your hand at making a paper chrysanthemum.

WHAT YOU NEED:

Florist's tape
Yellow construction paper
Green strip paper
Scissors
Pencil
Large needle
8" green pipe cleaner or
  florist wire
Glue

MAKE A PAPER CHRYSANTHEMUM:

1. Cut 4 4-inch circles of red, orange, or yellow paper. Cut a 2" x ½" strip of paper and set aside.

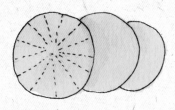

2. Draw a small circle (about ¼") in the center of each circle. Draw radiating lines to the edges.

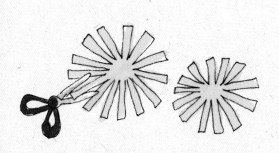

3. Cut along the radiating lines as closely as you can to the inner circle.

4. Take one circle and curl the tips of your fringe toward the center circle, as tightly as you can.
5. Curl the fringe of your remaining circles, each a little less tightly than the one before it.

6. Stack all your circles, placing the one with the tightest curls on top and the one with the loosest curls on the bottom.
7. Pierce the center of the stack with a large needle, making a small hole through the layers.

8. Thread a green pipe cleaner (or 8" of florist wire) through the needle hole.
9. Bend the tip of the pipe cleaner (inside the stack) so that it doesn't stick up or fall through the hole. Wrap with florist's tape.
10. Wrap the strip of paper around the base of your flower and glue in place to keep your flower from slipping down the stem.

Water Lantern Festival

The 15th Day of the 10th Lunar Month (November or December)

On this day at sundown, ancestors are remembered by the lighting of flower-shaped lanterns set afloat on streams or lakes. Traditionally, the day honored Emperor Yu, the Ruler of Water.

Winter Solstice Festival Dongzhi

The 7th Day of the 11th Month

This festival celebrates the Winter Solstice, the longest night of the year. After the solstice, the nights will grow shorter and the days longer.

It is a time of rest for workers, families, and officials, a time to exchange gifts and offer sacrifices to Heaven and ancestors, and of course to feast. People eat *tangyuan* served in a sweet broth. In Taiwan, people enjoy nine-layer cakes. They also make steamed cakes in the shape of chickens, ducks, tortoises, pigs, cows, or sheep. A grand banquet tops the day's activities.

Sweet Glutinous Rice Balls *tangyuan*
Colorful sticky and chewy balls sometimes stuffed with different fillings. You may want to try out the recipe on page 24.

The Sun Dial
Chinese astronomers determined the winter solstice over 2,500 years ago by observing the sun's movements with a sun dial, which uses the position of the sun's shadow as a way of telling and measuring time.

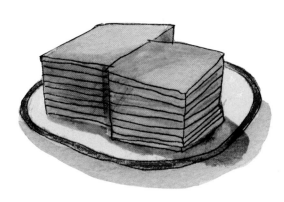

Nine-layer Cakes
Made with sugar and glutinous rice flour and steamed into a pastry to give as offerings

Steamed Cakes
Molded in the shape of auspicious animals

Laba Festival

8th Day of the 12th Lunar Month

This is a day to remember ancestors and also to honor Buddha by eating laba congee, a porridge made of rice, beans, dried nuts, and meat. The porridge is cooked for a long time and then first offered to ancestors, and then the family eats together at noon.

Birth of a Baby

Everyone in the family eagerly awaits the birth of a baby. A new life ensures the continuation of the family into the future. People like to tie lucky charms like gold bells on babies' wrists and ankles, or dress their feet in slippers embroidered with tigers, or stitch lucky coins into their clothing.

How Old is the Newborn?

A child is considered one year old on the day it is born because everyone grows a year older on the Lunar New Year, no matter what the birth date.

Count Your Age the Chinese Way

Give yourself one year on the day you were born. Add one year for every Spring Festival that follows after your birth date. A child born on New Year's Eve will be two years old two days after it was born!

1st Month Celebraion Manyue

One month after a baby is born, the family celebrates the occasion with a big feast to welcome the new member of the family. Guests give babies gifts such as clothing, and in return they receive a small red and yellow cake and hard boiled eggs painted red. The day after the gathering, the baby's hair is shaved off to make way for the growth of permanent hair.

Special Birthday Celebrations

Traditionally the Chinese don't pay much attention to birthdays except those for newborns and older people. People are proud of their age and start to really celebrate when they turn sixty. The 60th birthday marks the end of one life cycle and the beginning of the next. After that, a birthday celebration is held every ten years. The older the person is, the greater the celebration. According to tradition, the foods served have happy meanings. Long, uncut noodles and steamed dumplings in the shape of peaches signify a long life.

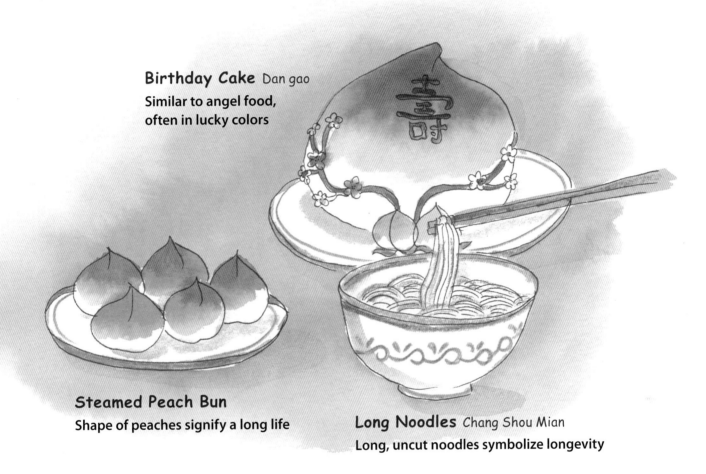

Birthday Cake Dan gao
Similar to angel food, often in lucky colors

Steamed Peach Bun
Shape of peaches signify a long life

Long Noodles Chang Shou Mian
Long, uncut noodles symbolize longevity

The Birthday Song

Happy Birthday to you!
zhù ni shēng rì kuài lè

Happy Birthday to you!
zhù nǐ shēng rì kuài lè

Happy Birthday to you!
zhù nǐ shēng rì kuài lè

Happy Birthday to you!
zhù nǐ yǒng yuǎn kuài lè

Weddings

On the morning of the wedding, the bride wakes up to a home decorated in red. She makes tea and serves her parents. In older times this was a gesture of farewell, for she would soon be leaving to join the family of her new husband. The ceremony is usually attended only by the couple's immediate families. Afterwards, the bride will serve tea to her new family.

The reception is a joyous affair. Family and friends share a nine or ten course meal. Chinese brides often change outfits at least three times during the reception.

Tea Ceremony

Meanwhile, the parents of the groom symbolically dress their son for the wedding. On the way to the ceremony, he and his parents stop at the house of the bride. The young couple serves tea to both sets of parents as a gesture of thanks and respect.

Red is the Traditional Color of Weddings

It stands for love, joy, and prosperity, and it appears in various ways in Chinese wedding traditions. Often it is the color of the bride's wedding gown, as well as the invitations, gift boxes, and envelopes for money. The double happiness sign captures the spirit of the day.

Nowadays many couples choose Western-style weddings. But some older traditions remain.

Wedding dates are carefully chosen to guarantee a good start in life.

A Year of Celebrations

We began this book at the end, when we celebrated the close of the old year. And now, many moons later, we end the book at the beginning, and celebrate all the years to come.

Published by Tuttle Publishing, an imprint of
Periplus Editions (HK) Ltd.

www.tuttlepublishing.com

Library of Congress Control Number: 2022945010

This edition ISBN 978-0-8048-4116-0

Distributed by
North America, Latin America & Europe
Tuttle Publishing
364 Innovation Drive
North Clarendon, VT 05759-9436 U.S.A.
Tel: (802) 773-8930
Fax: (802) 773-6993
info@tuttlepublishing.com
www.tuttlepublishing.com

Asia Pacific
Berkeley Books Pte. Ltd.
3 Kallang Sector, #04-01
Singapore 349278
Tel: (65) 6741-2178
Fax: (65) 6741-2179
inquiries@periplus.com.sg
www.tuttlepublishing.com

First edition

25 24 23 22
10 9 8 7 6 5 4 3 2 1

Printed in China
22010EP

"Books to Span the East and West"

Tuttle Publishing was founded in 1832 in the
small New England town of Rutland, Vermont
[USA]. Our core values remain as strong today as
they were then—to publish best-in-class books
which bring people together one page at a time.
In 1948, w established a publishing office in
Japan—and Tuttle is now a leader in publishing
English-language books about the arts, languages
and cultures of Asia. The world has become a
much smaller place today and Asia's economic
and cultural influence has grown. Yet the need
for meaningful dialogue and information about
this diverse region has never been greater. Over
the past seven decades, Tuttle has published
thousands of books on subjects ranging from
martial arts and paper crafts to language learning
and literature—and our talented authors,
illustrators, designers and photographers have
won many prestigious awards. We welcome you
to explore the wealth of information available on
Asia at www.tuttlepublishing.com.